Additional Praise for author, Bruce Piasecki's
next book
Conquering Tomorrow Too

D0255231

*I was unaware of Eileen Fischer's f̶... ... ... I read this
excellent chapbook on this quietly powerful legend. The thread-count
of business insights in her story is immeasurable. I like most how her
authentic personality fashions the purpose of her brand, especially
when she's going up against the big boys with her simple but vex-
ing Socratic question, "What is enough?" The Quiet Genius of Eileen
Fischer is a quick read with lasting inspiration. I look forward to the
full set of exemplar lives Bruce Piasecki has written about.*

– Park Howell, Founder, Business of Story

*Aristotle notes that role models are crucial for developing virtues.
Bruce Piasecki's compelling descriptions of "Six that Make a Difference"
dramatize models of virtuous leadership for our age where mastering
the complexity of everyday requires unprecedented collaborative skills.
Read this book. It will prove worthy for your tomorrow.*

– William M. Throop, Professor of Philosophy and
Environmental Studies, Former Provost of Green Mountain College

*This new book by Bruce Piasecki serves as a reference point for the
current and next few generations. Bruce Piasecki makes this new
world achievable this century.*

– Michael Spanos, Founder & Managing Director,
Global Sustain Group

*Most business leaders that we know are larger than life characters.
That is what's so deeply surprising about this new book by Bruce
Piasecki. What he explores is how modest, quietly spoken effective
people can have as significant an impact as some of their gregarious
counterparts. Many can learn from those that dare.*

– Richard Ellis, Vice President, Corporate Social Responsibility,
Walgreens Boots Alliance

SHIRES✿PRESS

P.O. Box 2200
Manchester Center, VT 05255
www.northshire.com

THE QUIET GENIUS OF
EILEEN FISHER

Paperback ISBN Number: 978-1-60571-527-8
Hardcover ISBN Number: 978-1-60571-528-8

Printed in the United States of America

THE QUIET GENIUS OF

EILEEN FISHER

Bruce Piasecki

**Achieving Social Cohesion
in a time of Distrust and Turmoil**

The Quiet Genius of Eileen Fisher is an advance excerpt
Bruce Piasecki's next book:
Conquering Tomorrow Today: Six Exemplar Lives

Hello Chapbook Readers—

We each have high points in our life, what the insurance executive and poet Wallace Stevens called "moments of sudden rightness." To date, my books have been published by the world's largest publishers. Today, I have decided to try something new. Direct sales. Direct inputs from you to me at Bruce@ahcgroup.com.

The goal, now that I am 65, is to earn more inputs from my readers. Goodbye, for now, mainstream publishers. To me, today's big twenty commercial publishers seem mostly interested in publishing books of celebrities. This chapbook series is far different. I write about people like you and me, whose impact and consequence astounds.

During the 19th century, most writers, like Charles Dickens, enjoyed larger audiences through shorter, monthly entries. During the 20th century, my supercharged superhero, George Orwell, wrote a short series called *As I Please* that still astounds. They are greater writers than I, but why not follow these step-by-step paths?

Biographies in today's world are, at times, simply too heavy to lift. Take John Bolton's 2020 heavyweight on all the wrong things he witnessed in the life of Trump. Too long! That is a book few will actually finish, and many of us want to forget. These lives are exemplar, worthy of study.

Why This Chapbooks Series:

In this series, I've written about six lives of consequence, exemplar lives of immense social value- that have made an impact in our world now constrained by social unrest and serious in-fighting.

These six people helped me feel more hopeful about the future. They taught me social leadership skills that I had not yet attained from competitive basketball, or even from running my own firm for several decades.

Imagine, my new friends, what they might do for you.

Yours,
Bruce Piasecki

P.S. You can write Marti Simmons, a veteran Vice President at my management consulting firm, if you wish to arrange a discussion on any of these cases in the chapbook series. I am open to talking with you even if you are not a member of the press. My current goal is immediacy and impact. Eventually, I will absorb your inputs to write a summary book for a commercial press on Wealth and the Commonwealth.

Marti can be reached at marti@ahcgroup.com and 518-583-9615.

Preface and Overview

I am glad I got to see Bruce's latst book, *Conquering Tomorrow Today: Six Exemplar Lives,* before you in its early stages. I attended some of Bruce Piasecki's workshops as he was developing these chapbooks into *Conquering Tomorrow,* and met through the years several of those featured in this collection of smart profiles.

As we enter this third decade of the new millennium, it is clear that we are swimming in unchartered waters. That is why Piasecki calls this, in his classic 2007 book, a "swift and severe world." You see the sample book case study here on Eileen Fisher.

Every facet of our life – from the economy to politics to the natural environment – has become more volatile, uncertain, complex and ambiguous. Some call this complex "the age of VUCA." Piasecki calls this an age of mistrust, mischief and turmoil. This book examines how to get past this age.

Life has become **more volatile**, because interests are shifting across the world, accelerated by technology and new geopolitics; **more uncertain**, because of shifting societal expectations, mass inequality and the impacts of climate change; **more complex**, because of the growing interdependence of the economy, society and the environment in a global world; and **more ambiguous**, because our traditional governance and power structures are unfit for this new age.

At GlobeScan, we study these social shifts in world view from our offices in Brazil, Canada, Europe, Singapore and elsewhere, tabulating billions of inputs. Strangely enough, Bruce Piasecki's findings echo these larger trends from his personal observations of world views and the behavior of firms. Yet, while underlining the importance of our findings, he also gives us a way up and out into the 21st Century. His trends diagnostic is presented as solutions, and paths of discovery.

We have faced other significant challenges throughout history, from war to political scandal to economic calamity, and more often than not, have found our way through them.

When times are difficult, we have looked to that uniquely human property to help us navigate our way through disruption: leadership.

Enlightened, inspired and thoughtful leadership

This is a precious resource which we must cultivate and encourage as it has the potential to mobilize solutions to create a better future. It is in this context that I am so grateful for Bruce Piasecki's important book.

The timeliness of this book is in helping us learn from remarkable leaders and finding ways to apply their insights and experiences to many aspects of our lives, so we all become better and more effective leaders.

This book's subtitle - "How Wisdom Survives Chaos." I find aptly captures the urgency of better leadership to build consensus and trust. We need these six types of leaders and their bold actions to get us to the future we want. **In this age of polarization and declining trust in institutions,** we need leaders who can help our societies heal and work together to tackle the extraordinary challenges before us. These exemplar lives do exactly that, case by case.

The six people featured in Bruce's book – Linda Coady, Eileen Fisher, Frank Loy, Jack Robinson, John Streur and Steve Percy – provide powerful, even colorful, profiles of leadership. I have had the honor and good fortune to have met some of these remarkable individuals and have followed their careers. In Bruce Piasecki's hands, these individuals come alive for many, as they should.

These six come from very different walks of life. They represent a diverse array of sector experience including government, energy, fashion and finance. Yet, as you will see as you devour these books, they all share a passion for embracing complexity and leading with purpose. Further, they all have demonstrated the power of that indispensable leadership quality: **listening**.

These remarkable six individuals have repeatedly shown the **value of deep listening**, engagement and patient consensus building to affect real change. As Piasecki shows with wit and historic insights, we have a great deal to learn from them in this anxious age of turmoil and distrust.

Here at GlobeScan, I have a privileged vantage point through my work to see how expectations of stakeholders and the general public across the world are shifting in response to all of the challenges we face.

By happy circumstance, GlobeScan has worked for years for some of Bruce Piasecki's global management consulting clients. We do the empirical work; Piasecki and his team of lawyers and former executives refine the strategy once inside a given firm like Merck or Toyota or Walgreens.

While there is growing dissatisfaction to the status quo and heightening anxiety to the environmental crisis unfolding around us, especially among young people, **there is also a deep thirst for new approaches** in the way we live, work, consume, produce and collaborate.

Relating this Book to the Rest of our World

As we look into the next decades, it is critical that corporations shape their strategies and public responses in fulfillment of the United Nation's Sustainable Development Goals in 2030. These 17 goals (with a total of 169 targets) were developed collectively by governments, civil society and business and represent the best definition of the future we all want. They cover aspirational goals such as the end of poverty and hunger, access to proper education and health care, gender equity, and much more.

Together, they represent an integrated and renewed approach to how we can live, work and play. At times these seem overwhelming; yet, in the hands of this gifted writer, they are made more intelligible thru the lives of the six studied by Piasecki.

With all this in mind, these are timely books for our age.

Mixing all the best of Bruce's instincts and experience – knowing the key issues of our day and the stakes involved, having a keen understanding and appreciation of the historical context and showcasing, with a generous spirit, the lives of leaders that can teach us a better way forward.

Some of the critical answers for the new leadership lie within the experiences and stories of these special six. We are all better for having their lives so wonderfully and enthusiastically documented by Bruce Piasecki.

I will end with a few lines from Bruce himself, as I think they perfectly set us up for learning about Linda, Eileen, Frank, Jack, John and Steve. Piasecki notes:

> "Back in the 19th century, when there were so fewer people, great thinkers thought about what is humankind's role in changing the face of the earth. Now a mere 200 years later, we ask what is humankind's role in making this humanized planet sustainable."

Come meet this wonderful set of people.

Chris Coulter
CEO, GlobeScan
Canada, Brazil, United States, Singapore

Preface
Personality and Social Cohesion

You are about to meet six of the world's most extraordinary personalities—down to earth and humble people who have redefined what it means to succeed in business and excel in society. For decades, they have navigated through the world's largest corporations and powerful governments, redirecting how these giants operate and impact the world. And most likely, you have never heard their names before.

Why write biographies of people who are largely unknown? I've been asked this question countless times: by friends, family, editors, and colleagues. By the very people profiled in this book.

Here is a reason:

These six personality types have proven prescient on how to compete in today's swift and severe world. In addition, these six people offer you a way to make your own life more consequential.

I have read books like this before.

I remember from college, vividly, Vasari's book on Italian Painters, where you got a glimpse of the essence of the painters in action. Then, during graduate studies, there was Sigmund Freud's early case study work; and then, in the last decade, my favorite by far, Winston Churchill's colorful account of his acquaintances in Great Contemporaries. In this collection, Winston Churchill brought alive personalities such as Lawrence of Arabia long before anyone knew of them.

These interesting short biographies are not written with monumental detail. This is a compositional choice I made, to be sure to get you a sampling of six rather than death by historic details on one. life That is why we offer you here short lively accounts of the essence of someone you'd find curious. While ordinary people, they are given force and grave by society. And it is preciously through their personalities that they inspire loyalty, respect and one of the rarest remaining social amenities of today, social cohesion.

Let me explain what I mean by social cohesion

These personalities are gifted at making the patterns of today meaningful and believable rather than confused. Instead of gaining strength through turmoil and distrust, they help society cohere. There is a stunning coherence in what they do. We need them today in our most turbulent world more than ever. Our world filled with police brutality, carbon and capital constraints, and constant political bickering seems beyond calm, beyond resolution. Until you watch what these lives do.

Dacher Kellner gets to the core of what makes these lives matter in this opening passage to his book, *The Power Paradox*:

> "Life is made up of patterns. Patterns of eating, thirst, sleep, and fight or flight are crucial to our individual survival; patterns of courtship, sex, attachment, conflict, play, creativity, family life, and collaboration are crucial to our collective survival. **Wisdom** is our ability to perceive these patterns and to shape them into **coherent chapters** within the longer narrative of our lives. In this way, wisdom survives crisis. That is what is needed this decade, and those decades ahead."

Yes, we can say the six I've chosen to spend three years writing about are what constitute acts of wisdom. That is what I am dramatizing here—their state of wisdom. I am not offering exactly how they won a case or made a business decision. I provide essential sketches, not exhaustive how-to learning here, for I do not really believe what the future needs is more manuals. What the future needs is the cultivation of the skills you can glean from meeting these six. You may be malicious, you may be altruistic, you may be neither. What matters is how effective you can become in line with the principles found in their lives.

Like surfers in a lasting storm, these six business and social leaders know **why they are out there**. Their lives have proven meaningful to far more than themselves, their families and their friends. I ask, "How did that happen?"

Saratoga Springs, New York
Summer of 2020
Written after a month of racial tensions exploded by the death of George Floyd.

The Quiet Genius of Eileen Fisher

Eileen Fisher's elusive genius creates an atmosphere of contemplative privacy around her. Her quiet genius has helped create a profitable brand in the fashion world. She is as much an icon, a legend, as a person who provides fabrics and dresses to buy.

She does not flaunt that legendary status, in fact, she acts somewhat shy about it. There is an eloquent simplicity to her designs and products; in the course of this essay, you will see how Eileen Fisher works her genius.

I never met Eileen Fisher for this essay. I have watched her in investment meetings; in public settings, in dozens of videos and social media events. Yet I never needed a one on one conversation with her to notice the quiet in her genius.

I met many who knew her, and dozens that work for her.

I chose to write about Eileen because I found her executive style stunning. She was a new kind of executive for me; someone very different from those I've spent a life with. I had heard of her legend for decades, when I first watched her in action down in Manhattan at www.cecp.co. You can watch this video on Chief Executive for Corporate Purpose. I must say I am glad I did not meet her. Her magic is legendary. The legend of Eileen Fisher resides in her organization and in each fabric design and each store.

⚶

Irving Berlin lived a long luxurious Manhattan-based life, a life in the public eye. He is perhaps most famous for saying "The toughest thing about success is that you've got to keep on being a success." New Yorkers are known for these informed double zingers that rip through your head.

I had thought of Berlin's even patterned pieces when I heard Eileen Fisher speak other times in public, and through dozens of recordings on YouTube and her extensive showing on company web pages. There is something soft and mesmerizing yet insistent about her voice, her stance. When you hear such a voice, you wonder if this played a part in making her so admired before she became this legend.

She is famous in her realm, and more lasting than any living fashion designer. You knew her stance on properly sourced fabrics for the last twenty years. My firm knew her statements about sustainability for a quarter century. Whitney Bauer writes extensively in *Fashionista* about how Eileen has been sustainable before it was "buzzy," explaining her Social Innovation Projects and her positions announced at the Parson's annual benefit in 2017. But close watchers like Bauer know "the brand was incorporating sustainable practices since 2000, when it introduced its first organic yoga pant. Social responsibility became a priority even earlier, as addressing human rights issues within the supply chain became paramount for Eileen Fisher in the 1990s."

The Legend and The Person

I have brought you back now to the beginning of the book. For here, alone, stands Eileen Fisher, well-dressed before the big hall of investors and the other CEOs. Here she is speaking from her soul, before a group of over 150 investment houses, with several CEOs in the room, as part of this Chief Executive for Corporate Purpose event.

She is wondering out loud about some shortcomings in the "CEOs talk." She asks the rather masculine CEO of Johnson and Johnson after his 55 minutes speak one question, then sits down gracefully: "Sir, may I ask: What is enough?"

She has asked this profound question, often ignored in the halls of modern capitalism, both of herself and of her firm. After success, she converted the corporation in her name into an Employee Stock Ownership Plan (ESOP). She is far more generous than the norm to her staff and her executives.

Eileen Fisher, The company, makes cash contributions to the ESOP on a consistent periodic basis based on overall performance. For instance, the

2017 cash contribution to every worker at the firm amounted to $1,100. In addition, the ESOP offers a traditional 401K retirement plan, and the company distributes a large portion of their pre-tax profits back to their employees in end of the year variable bonuses. Like a commonsensical gift-giver, these bonuses are handed out every December before the holidays.

This is part of the legend, and exceptional. How many law firms, or management consulting firms like the one I founded, can demonstrate these steps beyond bald self-interest?

In contrast, most self-made corporate leaders activate Ann Rand's *The Virtue of Selfishness*. They remain devoted to its worldview except in the pursuit of tax benefits and personal tax deductions, in general. Most pursue policies of endlessly expansive markets. Unilever's CEO Paul Pohlman, for example, another popular speakers in the Chief Executive Forum is noted to be a rock star of sustainability. Yet in fact their companies censor anything that constrains global consumerism. Unilever sells products in 190 of the 195 nations on Earth with an effective abandon, some extremists note.

I would wager a bet that our entire equity culture is based on Walt Whitman's famous optimism: "All goes onwards and upwards, nothing collapses, and to die is different than anyone supposed, and luckier."

Eileen Fisher, instead, asks: "What is enough?" and she means it. Her legend rests on opposing aspirations, a set of beliefs far more uncommon and complex.

What Motivates This Team Called Eileen Fisher?

Reviewing the well documented and disclosed financial numbers across the last 12 years (2008-2020), the enterprise Eileen Fisher is not simply about the money. She runs a social enterprise within the corporation. What motivates Eileen and her talented staff is best thought of as a creative enterprise first, and foremost.

We have before us a social and a corporate competitor that defines a transformational sense of leadership. In the first two years I studied her actions I incorrectly attributed these features to a feminine mystique about competitiveness. When she first refused my direct attempts at interviewing her, I came to respect her elusiveness. Now I see it as part of a larger consistent pattern in her way of doing business. There is a quiet genius to Eileen Fisher.

I read everything I can get in my hands about her and her key deputies. During my interviews of her top executives, I thought often about Janet Malcolm's brilliant *New Yorker* tribute to Eileen Fisher. It was written several years before I saw Fisher in action. Janet has been writing well-written and unhurried pieces for the *New Yorker* since 1963, so you would expect she treated Fisher with the skills and respect of a veteran. Malcolm's study is a superb example of journalist tact and respect.

Janet Malcolm did ask Eileen about what she thought of her mother. Eileen said one word: "Crazy." You can sense the veteran journalist Janet Malcolm was startled. Malcolm writes at the start of *Nobody's Looking at You: Eileen Fisher and the Art of Understatement:*

> "There is a wish shared by women who consider themselves serious that the clothes they wear look as if they were heedlessly flung on rather than anxiously selected. The clothes of Eileen Fisher seem to have been designed with the fulfillment of that wish in mind. Words like 'simple' and 'tasteful' and colors like black and grey come to mind along with images of women of a certain age and class for whom the hiding of vanity is an inner necessity."

This captures the solemnity of purpose in her shops.

A Set of Questions Before
We Get to Her Sense of Style

Every time I went into one of her stores with my wife, Andrea Masters, I would watch Andrea and the other women pause, evaluate, and buy. Part of the pleasure was watching them evaluate the simple touch of the fabrics, and how they fell on their features.

Here again in 2018, before Daryl Brewster, CECP's CEO, and Mark Tulay, and his network of 150 investment houses, the crowd around Eileen then were mostly well off Upper East Side professionals.

At least a third of that audience were, in fact, Upper East Side professionals. The others, a set of well-known investment Heads and corporate executives that probably would live in the Upper East Side if it made sense financially. Here was Eileen, a successful, comfortable, firm female executive, the founder and CEO of her firm, saying two magic words I seldom hear in business circles: "Enough" and "Crazy."

Those from the Upper East Side, and those from the investment houses, shy away from those words wholeheartedly, in general, and especially in group settings. Yet they keep going to buy in her stores.

After several years of looking into Eileen Fisher's record as an achiever and as a firm, I began to ask questions that are rooted in something deeper than her person. Has she made a firm that uniquely captures her sense of social history?

Suddenly, as if locked in a foreign taxi ride, I wanted to know what she wanted to do next with her extraordinary life. The questions just flowed from this early defiant public image she projected, with such few words, as soon as I left her as a real person and began asking about the genius of her firm.

I spoke with the literary agent of my last six books. He said this shift to her firm on my part was good. You can say I rapidly developed "an inner necessity" to meet this creative, seemingly less repressed, executive. I was attracted to writing about the large margin of profitability in her firm. But I discerned early that I was more interested in writing about her, the character, the person, and the legend rather than just a typical business case study of leadership. I developed my list of primary questions:

1.   Was it that her success had simply made her less repressed when it comes to the usual bombast and CEO gestures at greatness?

2.   Did she always display a personal gravitas from youth (yes, it appears)?

3.   Did she have something different going into the mix of the fashion industry, so often based on a sense of style. Was it simply: Drive? Ambition? Wit? Self-control? Indirect aggression against manhood itself? Sport?

These questions cannot be answered, unfortunately, as she puts up a wall of protection between what she inspires in staff and buyers, and what she has chosen as her responsibility to explain or not to explain.

In a way, it was like trying to deal with the head of a superpower nation. They had plenty of better things to do, and as many more to avoid. By the end of year three in study of her firm, I gave up on gaining actual access. The full-throated interview would not occur, her head of press told me in 2019. I had already shared drafts, and she felt I had completed "the heavy lifting" without needing to meet Eileen herself, who was deeply engaged in starting a new set of initiatives to start 2020.

Some Contrast in Her Personality

The first thing I wanted to be sure about when deciding to explore a legend rather than an actual person was the question of authenticity. Was Eileen Fisher the firm as authentic as Eileen Fisher the founder and top executive? This was an important question, as her firm's high costs are based on this feeling of authenticity.

I did not find Eileen Fisher anything but robustly authentic, sportively self-controlled. There was no funny business in her fun business.

She was not like Gary Hart in any sustained way. When I had interviewed Gary Hart as a Senator before his decision to run for President; I found a smart, reserved intellectual. Regarding Eileen Fisher, I had seen some similar attributes of leadership, even companionship, in her behavior and business moves. But by the end of the third year of studying her firm, I knew for sure there were more dissimilarities than similarities. She was more different (Crazy) than similar than the five others studied in these chapbooks. We live in a Brand New World, as Scott Bedbury, has studied in his book.

One thing was now clear by 2020, after finishing the case studies on Frank Loy, Steve Percy, and Linda Coady, Eileen Fisher was a strange special kind of CEO and Founder, far more private than most. She was, as Dawn Rittenhouse will soon explain, an effective introvert working on a very large and public canvas.

I went back and reread everything I had collected on introverts. Janet Malcolm, either due to her editors, or due to her respect of this high princess of fashion, did not probe these essentially private features of Eileen Fisher.

Appreciate Inquiry and Polite Questioning

Maybe it is even wrong to use the word "private" and "introvert." They usually connote elements of non-achievers, people note recognized as having done something bold with their lives.

Maybe the better word for her achievements would be "engage in a polite inquiry?" That is what actually one of her gatekeepers asked from me in 2019 before I was to gain access to her. "Bruce, can you engage in a polite inquiry? She is really into the theories of appreciative inquiry."

So that was one strong prerequisite before entry into Fisher-land. I told them I could not guarantee politeness, only professionalism. I felt the slow drawing close of a vault door, in response.

Stepping Back and Refusing Her Refusal

As I was writing the other cases in these books, I remained very positive about her firm. The magic in her growth and brand might be lost on some who fall for her mystique. But her results are based on exceptional financial numbers. In 2002, for example, the company earned $144 million in revenue, then $154 million in 2003. My daughter was a mere 6 and 7 years old in 2003, the years of wonder. But then by 2015, Eileen Fisher earned a revenue of over $300 million. A doubling in 12 years, about the rate of weight growth in my daughter. Astonishing for a mature firm.

I am almost certain that Linda Coady, John Streur and Frank Loy were a lot more communicative with staff and stakeholders than Eileen Fisher, whose firm has a legendary set of pluses when it comes to corporate disclosure and stakeholder engagement and human rights.

Do we attribute such growth to Eileen Fisher's hire of brilliant deputies? Probably. When the firm goes from an exclusive American structure to opening stores in Vancouver and British Columbia, it seems sensible—

she is moving the West Coast wealth up north to smart rich buyers. This is business savvy at its best. But when she opens doors in London, the Middle East, what are we to think about her 56 global locations?

Clearly, there is something crazy and risk taking about Eileen Fisher the person, as well as the firm, that deserves placement in this book. Her means of dealing with the turmoil and mistrust of the modern world may be hidden, but they are certainly effective.

One Crazy CEO

At the end of a book like this, I request that the reader let me reflect back on the near two hundred CEOs I've interviewed in my work. Now 65, I realize our teams have completed management consulting assignments for more than 128 different organizations in forty years. But nothing caused me to question myself as much as this study of Eileen Fisher. Some folks in my firm are beginning to refer to me as a CEO, a title I resisted for decades, as I wanted to remain the Founder.

Back in the early 1990s, I had the privilege of writing about Lod Cook, the CEO of ARCO, the petroleum giant in Los Angeles, for the *Los Angeles Times*. He was classic, a strong outspoken male CEO. As you entered Lod's office at the end of last century, there was the usual long hallway of oil giants.

His SVP of public and government affairs, Kenneth Dickerson, a man who would join my firm after retiring from ARCO and its sale to BP, said as he was walking me in: "I feel like these naked Greek statues you are walking past when I am under Lod's gaze in my performance reviews. He does not miss a detail, Bruce. Why, Bruce, did you write about Lod as one crazy CEO?"

Sometimes the truth hurts, but sometimes the truth helps you get places as a writer. Over the years, you learn how to sneak into settings of interest, sometimes through understatement, sometimes it takes overstatement. In other words, gaining access to a CEO or Founder requires a range of tricks. But, in general, you learn that entry is key, as are first impressions of how you present yourself to their handlers.

The story of Eileen Fisher confirms this is also true to the world of design and fashion. Fashion continually requires tricks of entry. Most industries, like petroleum or chemicals, have large established barriers of entry that they keep less endowed beginners out. In fashion, there are not many barriers of entry. All Eileen really has is her legend, and the ability to reinvent the appeal of her legend. When you read the fashion magazines, fashion itself is often about new entries. What has enabled Eileen Fisher to outlast this ceaseless emphasis on startups for so long, now three decades at the highest levels of competition? In summary, I have experienced what Eileen Fisher's gatekeepers wanted me to feel. It wasn't about me. It was not about them. It was not about her. It was about her legend.

The Desire to Write About Her Nonetheless

I began to think: perhaps there is a kind of consumer's resentment when others see her as a bit crazy. Capitalism itself had made this word "enough" almost obsolete.

I concluded this phase of the research with this in mind: it is far easier to feel the vast universe of consumer delights sane than to question them. We are talking about a different kind of talent here, not a maker of iPads, or kids' bands. Most modern industry segments rely on the assumption that consumers all need enough excess, extra CDs they never return to, electronics that pile up in a corner full of over promise and waste. Eileen charges enough so you would truly prize her possessions.

Eileen is a different premium brand and would never thrive in the entertainment business. Eileen Fisher's career illustrates a quiet Thoreauvian condemnation of the declarations of excess. The modern predicament of success can be questioned in the very ways she cuts her cloth.

Eileen Fisher's Global Reach

Eileen Fisher clothing is sold at stores in these countries:

Canada (14)
Great Britain (9)
Ireland
Israel
South Africa
United Arab Emirates

Eileen Fisher has Stores in the Following US Locations:

Arizona
California (9)
Colorado
Connecticut (2)
Florida (6)
Illinois (3)
Maryland (2)
Massachusetts (6)
Michigan
Minnesota
Missouri (2)
New Jersey
New Mexico
New York (12)
North Carolina

Ohio
Oregon
Pennsylvania (2)
Tennessee
Texas
Vermont
Virginia
Washington (4)

Confronting the American Tradition: Going Global

In the American strain there had been so many others that got on this high horse of "enough." They usually are ignored by the mainstream of American capitalism. It is easy enough to think of the eloquence of Henry David Thoreau, or the screeching certainties of Bill McKibben's ominous relentless prose. But I sensed something new here in our case of Eileen Fisher and her firm: **the "enough" questions came from Eileen with a sense of luxury.** I had only seen this once before in my travels for Toyota through Japan.

Perhaps her chronicler Janet Malcolm was onto something when she wrote: "I remember going into the Eileen Fisher shops that were opening around the city in the late nineteen-eighties.... I was attracted by the austere beauty of the clothes. They were loose and interesting. There was an atmosphere of early modernism in their geometric shapes and murky muted colors." **Japan is full of austere beauty of this kind.** There was nothing really sexy nor surprising in this description by Malcolm. It is accurate.

However, I began to feel this reading of the Eileen Fisher brand inadequate. Thoreau is very much an American anti-dote. In sharp contrast, Eileen Fisher is a global hit. At this time of writing she has become a truly global phenomenon. (See chart on page 29). My researchers had to construct this chart because she is clearly not wanting many to know how global she has become. Very few Americans know how global Eileen Fisher has become.

How does Eileen Fisher's global reach relate, then, to a global oil executive? They both operate 24/7, with aligned staff situated in a thoughtful global way? This enables, with intelligent staffing, success in many different cultures and family types. Perhaps more than *The New Yorker* editor's expected when they first presented Eileen Fisher as a quintessential New Yorker. Eileen Fisher, in my reading, is more like Lod Cook, or an oil executive. She is more elusive than any oil executive I've ever met or worked with.

Take, for instance, Eileen's efforts to turn reclaimed garments into an economically viable collection of renewed, fashionable, and remade clothing globally. She first tried this out in Irvington, New York, about an hour north of Manhattan, ground zero, near her actual home. Here is where she laid the foundations of a new way of thinking, in a fashion similar to how the oil giants I've worked for have thought through their supply chains. To do this from New York is completely unexpected, as New York remains the haven of waste in fashion and fashion design.

Why This Concern
About Recycled Fabrics

After the Ellen MacArthur Foundation published a touchy account of how less than one percent of material used in producing garment globally is recycled, Eileen Fisher had had enough. This happened in about the year 2010, as issues like climate change and plastics in the oceans matured before the public's hemlines.

Eileen Fisher then realized through this report, and others internally commissioned more recently, that 87 percent of total fiber content is incinerated or sent to landfills rather than reused. Her smart deputies calculated this loss worth about $100 billion or more in a year. Eileen took action in her hometown of Irvington. I actually was sent a copy of this financial breakdown from a fellow competitor of Eileen's, another female owner made sure I did not leave her out in telling this tale.

Today, Eileen Fisher has collected over 960,000 garments for recycling or resewing in what they all call up there "The Tiny Factory." They have one in Seattle as well and are exploring the concept globally in the 2020s. This has opened Eileen's line to a younger generation.

She also donates some to women's shelters, art schools, and disaster relief efforts. This is how oil executives act during boon years; but Eileen adds a strong stable steadiness to this, as she does not pull back after offering social goods to her staff or society. I have not noticed significant losses during the pandemic, as her internet marketing unit is solid and global.

This view on waste is a key part of what I've been writing about for decades as "social response capitalism," where business leaders compete on price, quality and social needs. Eileen Fisher is the first to take this form of competition thus far in clothing.

Furthering the Analogue
to an Oil Giant

Well into her 60s, Eileen Fisher is exploring things in new ways. She knows when to think, when to act, when to remain invisible.

After reading my piece back then in *The Los Angeles Times*, CEO Lod Cook called me up directly one late Friday afternoon. That kind of frontal approach works for many males in power. They do not have time for anything less efficient. They often assume a brusque, abrupt style, even when talking to journalists or book writers. They assume you are already interested in them.

Eileen Fisher may assume the opposite here: What do I get from additional press? In one of her 2018 web page announcements, her branders say: "We acknowledge that profits are important to the success and growth of the company but no more important than our people and our planet." Of course, this triple bottom line concept is not her own, and its author, John Elkington, is looking to push the orientation for its next 25 years in a current blog.

An oil giant can never say this, as their entire enterprise is centered on a non-renewable stream of black gold. But listen to how Eileen Fisher, the brand, positioned this when they announced VISION 2020 in their March 2015 materials:

> "Our goal is contingent upon eight categories: materials, chemistry, water, carbon, conscious business practices, fair wages and benefits, worker voice, and worker and community happiness."

Her voice is soft, penetrating, but acceptable and circuitous in its persuasion. You see this strange mix of paradoxes in Noh and Kabuki theatre.

At this point my readers should know she is neither a brusque Lod Cook kind of CEO, nor a refined Eastern lawyer-like CEO Kenneth Frazier of Merck. She is not easily characterized, or boxed in. You can think of her as a wildcatter with 1,100 employees.

Trapped Before I Started

Listen to how Eileen's people write about one of the most sensitive and explosive CEO issues of the day, diversity and inclusion: "Our workforce demographics show that while women make up 84 percent of our employee population, they make up 77 percent of our leaders (director and above). It is our challenge, and opportunity, to bring the gender composition of our leadership closer to that of our entire employee community. In addition, 35 percent of our employee population identifies as persons of color, while 20 percent of our leaders (director and above) identify as persons of color."

The firm is a strong advocate for the Family Leave Act. They transported employees to attend the Women's March on Washington at the company's expense. They have consistently participated with community organizations that have a strong focus on human rights and the empowerment of women and girls.

No other firm is close to these numbers in the big 500. And most of the big 500 say that Eileen's numbers are unattainable.

That is a way of suggesting: Perhaps Eileen is not crazy. Perhaps the dominant culture is? Maybe she found a more reliable source of creativity in the mix of staffers she found before her. Perhaps I am open to this suggestion since I was raised by women, with an ever-present grandmother from Poland, a single factory mother, and a biological older sister and a foster Chinese American sister. Eileen's 1,100 people represent the color and texture of the new world.

Talking More to Her Staff

I talked with dozens of people outside her organization about her, and a dozen within. They gave me a sense of this master.

Everyone in her firm is instructed to call her Eileen, on a first name basis. I do not feel it even appropriate to quote, in most cases, anything but the first names of the sources within her firm. They are consistently articulate, well-paid professionals speaking on behalf of Eileen. If I was frustrated by rejection, I would call her professionals "perfect cyborgs" as one of my political journalist friends calls the polite distancing gatekeepers in Washington these days. The outside sources on Eileen Fisher do have perspective, but that is usually tainted by competitive jealousy.

You find a nice balance of inside and outside in Eileen Fisher's "Annual Benefit Corporate Report for Fiscal Year 2019." It is all posted, all branded with clean well-designed pages and third-party verified numbers. In Eileen's empire, there is a difference between having a traditional corporate training record, and being a person, a whole interesting person, worthy of a spot on the team.

Once they land the job, the appreciation warrants a special kind of loyalty and magic. Talking with a few Human Resource professionals, and Diversity and Inclusion consultants, it seems Eileen needs to feel you were born into the Fisher family.

My lifelong friend and Diversity expert Dr. Ilene Wasserman of Philadelphia said, "You are ready to tackle someone like Eileen Fisher, Bruce. Your wife rewired you enough." Again, that word "enough."

Open Disclosure and Public Branding

Here is what DuPont's former global sustainability leader, Dawn Rittenhouse, says about Eileen Fisher and her career as a leading change maker in a massive and historic chemical giant:

> "In 2012, when the book *Quiet* was published, I found it refreshing to read about the leadership style of introverts. The book shows me, and the corporate world, how introverts can be as powerful as extroverts....Every day we encounter extroverts and leaders that are charismatic. But it is hard to find those leaders that do not seek the spotlight yet make a real difference in the world...."

I have never had the opportunity to meet Eileen Fisher. I have had meetings with her staff, in their offices in Manhattan, to discuss human rights issues with them in the supply chain. From these meetings, it was clear to me that Eileen's organization goes beyond the mainstream in approaching what is necessary, but furthers that normative approach with much more, some of which is completely unannounced. I believe this mindset started at the top from Eileen Fisher herself. Eileen has not been out there raising a flag about how to do sustainable business, she is instead leading an organization that shows you can be successful and more responsible past the mainstream. I have thought about that often as I approach how I do my work."

—Dawn Rittenhouse, Former Director, Sustainable Development, DuPont Global

Since Eileen Fisher's organization is intelligently open, leaving a trail of acts on their financial reports, annual reports, web-pages and marketing brochures, you can confirm everything Dawn Rittenhouse said.

Another telling interview was with Mark Tulay, the executive director of the Strategic Investment Initiative, a part of the CEO Force for Good network that we wrote about at the beginning of this essay when we met Eileen in public. Mark mentions the first time he heard Eileen speaking to his group of investors and CEOs. She quietly got to the podium, slowly looked out at the audience and bright lights and said:

> "There are a lot of men that look uncomfortable in their ties and suits out there. Perhaps I should add a men's line to our firm." Humor on top of directness hidden.

Hiding by Excelling

There are only a few more things to say about the quiet genius of Eileen Fisher. Malcolm sums up her persona brilliantly:

> "Eileen presented herself as someone who is still trying to overcome an innate awkwardness and shyness and verbal tentativeness. 'Speaking and writing has always been hard for me,' she said as her colleagues looked on fondly and encouragingly, as if at a relative with an endearing quirk."

Before closing this case, I talked to my book agent, Bob Diforio, about my decision to close the case on Eileen Fisher without ever meeting here eye to eye..... and he said:

> "There is a story there, so why not pursue these particular and peculiar themes. Draft what you've got with or without Eileen."

As the former CEO of New American Library, and head of an agent team that once sold a four-book deal for me in a week, I trust his sense of things worth pursuing strikes me as informed.

Finding the Founder's Beginnings

I reread several accounts of when Eileen first came to Manhattan as a young woman from the Chicago suburb of Des Plaines. She had come to New York to become an interior designer. This false start told me something about her determination.

Malcolm notes:

> "But she wasn't succeeding. 'I wasn't good with words,' she said. 'I wasn't that good with people, either. I couldn't explain my ideas to clients."

To support herself several sources have confirmed that she waited tables and took on freelance graphic design jobs until she met a Japanese man printing something at a shop.

Rei, the Japanese graphic designer, became a lover. They went to work in Japan at various advertising projects—from representing Kirin Beer to chemical companies and stationery companies. This youthful stage I call "preparatory experimentation stage." Eileen would probably call it "a turn in my life." I do not want to minimize this understatement. Shakespeare built his entire tragedy of King Lear on his daughter saying, "Nothing my Lord."

Over time the relationship frayed, when she realized he was treating her as a "little assistant." Japan enabled her now to feel inspired. She saw the kimono. How it was thrown around the woman in different ways. She left Japan and Rei with the kimono in her mind.

As the story is retold, after Rei, she next met a guy who was a sculptor in Tribeca. She now did all kinds of design work—some for apartments, some more stationery, mostly what she called "small things." She took out a booth with this sculptor who was making jewelry with her. Eileen, within a few months, took over the booth when the boyfriend stopped making jewelry. She had to share the space with two designers, not being able to afford the full booth.

Suddenly it was less than a month before one of the first pivotal shows. This is often in the tale described in the company literature as "the first show," but we have reason to believe there was, like in Walt Whitman's case, a longer foreground.

During all this time, Eileen never learned how to draw clothing designs formally. Like a talented musician that does not need to read music, she assembled her teams without knowing the inherited patterns. Instead, she hired someone to sew for her and make the first patterns. She kept thinking about the kimono. She could visualize the end garment in her mind now, but she needed others to transact her vision.

She guided the creation by words and gestures, more neck here, less fabric there. It was like how some write and rewrite or how many talents play music. A woman named Gail sewed the cloths. Eileen was in business.

Putting Some Threads Together

I took to the internet, where you can see many of her beautiful designs of high-end woman's clothing. There really is not that much recoverable "in words" from her first truly successful launch until close to 2010.

Almost two growing decades in relative silence.

Today you can see a massive amount of information about Eileen Fisher on her own web pages. She seems to be everywhere.

She has an entire LIFEWORK section on their web pages. Look for the "Women Together CONNECT" segments, an interactive live-stream experience with Eileen. The life notes section includes titles such as:

- **Change Can Be Hard:** A Tiny Practice for Self-Compassion
- Enjoy More: **Life After Overdrive**
- A Video called **Self-Care and Letting Ourselves off the Hook**
- **Calm and Present:** A Tiny Practice for Grounding

- **ENOUGH:** A writer's cure for perfection by Laura Kidyk

These are wonderfully engaging and informative. Consistently, they offer new creative takes on modern life. You cannot tell if any of the phrasing is Eileen's. But you can tell the stuff is far more sophisticated and thought out than, say, *Vanity Fair* or *Woman's Day*. Besides weaving together lovely fabrics, the new Eileen Fisher now explains a world view.

This is distinct for her industry. In a competitive fashion space that includes strong designer personalities like Carolina Herrera and Keerby Jean-Raymond, fantastic stylists like Mel Ottenberg, and plenty of other big sharks like Bergdorf Goodman's Linda Fargo, Eileen stands out in my mind for her original touch and now her world view.

A City Set on a Hill

Perhaps this is why Eileen Fisher was celebrated with Rihanna at the Neiman Marcus Parsons benefit recently. That honor came after nearly 30 years of consistent differentiation of product, with one overwhelming signature and style.

There are about 70 fashion and clothing design schools in the country, and several hundred more in the world, that teach the fundamentals of fashion design and delivery. My researchers visited a few. Eileen Fisher speaks to this new generation through videos and blogs that are branded by her staff. She is well known and respected in the 70 nodes of the future.

But she is the only Parson's Award recipient who used her acceptance speech to underline the importance of sustainability focused on social innovation. For those who do not know what sustainability has come to mean in modern business, this means Eileen is acknowledged by her peers as shaping the state of the art in making sure fashion has a long future in a carbon and capital constrained world.

As she scaled up, her products are now sold in the new century at a price that was not outrageous for two reasons. For more greedy companies, the pricing strategy upon success goes in the opposite direction. Superior doctors charge more, superior law firms have a better per diem, and management consulting firms no longer ask for work beneath an outrageous level.

How did she do this?

She had figured out a brilliant marketing strategy. Fractional store fronts. You never see this in successful law firms, management firms, or dentists. Easier, but not cheaper, to build a debt-free empire and control your space.

Fractional storefronts mean you team up with six or ten other designers, each paying a sixth or a tenth, and you get to put all the designer names on the front door and windows. This way people were coming to Eileen Fisher's grey to black eloquence more than the others, and she was not paying but a fraction of the floor prices.

What Is Enough?

Maria Bobila reported in *Fashionista* April of 2017, that "at 65, with three plus decades of fashion experience, the designer and newly named activist is more involved with her namesake label than ever." I would differ, and argue that her advocacy is not new. In my book, Eileen Fisher has argued to doing more with less and has asked the question "What is enough" with a profound consistency. She refined the tact with new discoveries in science, but the message is uniform: **calm down, think this through, stop wasting, do what is fundamental, do more with less.**

The women who wear Eileen Fisher's clothes are often accomplished professionals: lawyers, editors, public relations experts, psychotherapists, professors of all areas from women's studies to geology, staid doctors, and understated administrators with significant budgets. She also has a brilliant after market strategy, where the new generation of women can create her wardrobe at a discount.

Take, for example, Kathy Sierra. Kathy has had a most distinguished life, being the former head of the World Bank's human resources department. I met her when she was leaving her ultimate job at the World Bank, where she had assembled a 4 billion-dollar climate change infrastructure investment part of the Bank. She has served, brilliantly, one decade-long client of my firm as an effective part of the ten expert global advisory we had created and facilitate twice a year for the firm. I like Kathy Sierra very much. We talk family, we talk about the council. It is all very exacting.

But when she talks about the clothes of Eileen Fisher it all changes. Suddenly, there is a feeling of worthy luxury, a love of things not concepts, real admiration. Kathy says: "I have a closet full of Eileen's work. It makes me happy. I am originally from Spain, my deceased husband of Irish blood, but when you put on a Fisher you feel you can fit anywhere in the world. Being alone now, when I go to a fine restaurant, they may give me a bad seat next to the bathroom or another. I've begun to reserve for two, and when I am sitting at a fine table, say 'I am so sorry my husband will need to miss this meal.' Eileen's clothes give me that extra to navigate this world."

Someone is Looking at You

From these conversations with leaders like Dawn Rittenhouse and Kathy Sierra, I now offer a world view according to Eileen Fisher. This is really from crowd sourcing of the women executives in our Corporate Affiliates programs. Think of this as lessons without words from Eileen Fisher's way of being:

Love is a state of blissful confusion, between the real Rei, the wanted booth, and the marvelous results from team. Be alert to what you love.

Admiration, so much ruder, immediate, and deeper than corporate brand, requires many skills to earn. We admire what we can see and feel as authentic. That takes more than an MBA.

Luxury is not in the eye of the beholder. Luxury is real. It is a feeling based on freedom. It is a form of grace combined with freedom. It has little to do with the material world.

Coda

Here is the higher fact I am getting at, inspired by Eileen. Humans think and feel by analogue and visualization, not only by fact and fantasy. If we only lived in a world of science and engineering and medicine, we would not need Eileen Fisher, Frank Loy, Steve Percy, Linda Coady, and John Streur.

I argue we need them more than ever. These masters of social admiration, love, and care are the masters of our new forms of social response capitalism. This is the kind of capitalism that can answer the many challenges of tomorrow. This case underlines that there are many more things more important than profit.

In sum, money may not be what makes this world go around, especially for those like Eileen's staff who have a new glimpse of what is real in the workforce. That is the value in looking over Eileen Fisher's domain. In a sense, she is casting new light on the darkness of commercialism.

Eileen lets her folks think about their special pursuit of love, admiration and luxury, nearly every day. The hours are not exceedingly long, just smart. She is not only the artist type turned enterpriser and now a smart efficient systems builder.

She wants us to be artists, too, not just consumers. That may prove the tallest demand of Eileen Fisher.

"Hi Bruce. This is Marie Larson, Eileen's manager. Hope you had a lovely weekend. Really appreciate your enthusiasm around telling Eileen's unique story. At this moment in time, we are going to decline Eileen's participation. I realize you and the team would be doing a majority of the heavy lifting here. However, there are other priorities that we must fulfill first. Best of luck with the book."

—Marie Larson, EILEEN FISHER, Inc. She is the top PR manager at their offices at 111 Fifth Avenue in Manhattan.

It is late July, 2020 in Saratoga. Some of my sunflowers reached nine feet before opening up this year for the first time. These weeks have been lovely. My wife and I were rushed, after losing time in the garden. We rushed off to dinner, otherwise we would miss our anticipated movie *Leave No Trace*. "Pizza night," Andrea said.

We ate around the corner at a pizza joint founded 33 years ago by a high school couple. The man who thinks he is the sole owner and boss of this clean, well-designed restaurant still looks as good as he did when I first met him 20 years ago, no travel wear, still fit and firm. His co-owner wife, Sue, was wearing Eileen Fisher, when we met them by chance after the movies.

Note For Readers

You may detect something worthy of further inquiry in this case on Eileen Fisher. The person on her staff appointed to explain these paradoxes is Amy Hall, Eileen Fisher's director of social consciousness. If you Google Amy's name, talk with her directly, or talk with her colleagues, you get a person aware of the art scene, articulate in the nuance of plastics in the ocean, and the power in proper materials selection. While her title is social consciousness, she is physically astute of the material world. She says:

> "Eileen Fisher is committed to cracking up the very center of the fashion industry's supply chain. She strives to produce clothing that has a positive benefit to the earth—from seed to sewing machine."

Chapbook Snapshot: Eileen Fisher

- Asks "What is enough?"
- Authentic and self-controlled
- Global reach, moving beyond the mainstream in sustainability

Afterword

In Bruce Piasecki's exceptional 2007 book, *World, Inc.,* he wrote that "this book . . . identifies a pattern within capitalism that is larger than any specific example of good corporate leadership. It offers lasting concepts on how, within society itself, there are forces that are pushing capitalism into new forms and responsibilities." At the same time, in his management consulting work, Bruce began to expand discussions of corporate social responsibility to embrace the more pressing global problems of business growth and sustainability.

Bruce's next three books—*Doing More with Less: The New Way to Wealth* (2012), *Doing More with Teams: The New Way to Winning* (2014), and *New World Companies: The Future of Capitalism* (2016)—reflected the evolution of his management practice, from tactical planning to team management to the identification and delivery of world-class corporate performance.

Now comes a very different kind of book— *Conquering Tomorrow Today: Six Exemplar Lives: a study* of six accomplished people who are purpose driven, selfless, and deeply reflective. Through carefully wrought portraits, both intimate and evocative, Bruce depicts exceptional leaders, each with a unique blend of character and skill. Through these character studies, Bruce suggests how and why some firms succeed while others falter, by linking organizational achievement to the personalities of those who drive it.

Bruce explores the realm of leadership by life example. He does so by illuminating the lives of men and women whose influence extends far beyond their own firms—embracing staff, colleagues, customers, governments, and even markets. Thousands have been impacted, not only by what these leaders have done, but by how they have lived. Their example offers a message to all of us: we are often better than we realize. And, should we choose to embrace it, faith in who we are, and faith in others, often carries more weight than the entities we choose to serve.

This is the right time for such a series. First, these six lives exemplify the lessons of Julie Benezet's 2016 book, *The Journey of Not Knowing: How 21st-Century Leaders Can Chart a Course Where There Is None,* which explores the challenges of leading firms across uncharted territory and offers guidance on how to meet those challenges.

Piasecki reveals not only how these men and women have succeeded, but what it takes. As Bruce writes, his subjects have mastered the art of "advancing with dignity and result." All share five essential traits: **Uncompromising ethics, gifted dedication, compassionate insight, focused reflection,** and **uncommon civility**. Bruce offers us a uniquely personal perspective on the lives of leaders who are human—just like you and me—people whose lives we may have been curious about but never had the opportunity to see.

I predict his next book, *Conquering Tomorrow Today: Six Exemplar Lives*, will take their place among important readings in social biography, along with *The Wise Men: Six Friends and the World They Made* (Walter Isaacson and Evan Thomas, 1986), *Mirror to America: The Autobiography of John Hope Franklin* (2005), *Consider: Harnessing the Power of Reflective Thinking in Your Organization* (Daniel Patrick Forrester, 2011), *The Quartet: Orchestrating the Second American Revolution, 1783-1789* (Joseph J. Ellis, 2015), and *Jewish Justices of the Supreme Court: From Brandeis to Kagan* (David G. Dalin, 2017). As different as these books are, each offers a window into the minds of remarkable individuals who were at the center of complex and critical change.

As to who they are in our own subjective mirrors, these six are people who are often lost in histories dominated by either selfless circumstance, crises, and/or self-aggrandizing personalities who encourage their own cults.

Four of the six portraits incorporate a number of additional characters beyond the principal subjects. The resulting shifts in focus yield essential context that could not have been communicated without such a kaleidoscopic—if occasionally dizzying—view. The Eileen Fisher Chapbook is emotively and cerebrally as stunning as the Frank Loy. **In the latter there is brilliance. In the former there is genius.**

Bruce is an accomplished advocate of conscious and socially balanced investment within a framework of clarity rather than charity; of sustainable, long-term yields rather than short-term gains. In his view, personal success is not enough: we must lead others to success.

And to do that, we must understand why we lead, and what is required of those whom we trust to lead.

A practitioner and facilitator as well as a close observer of executive behaviors, Bruce continues to evolve as a social historian, futurist, and strategist, combining the prescience and narrative skill of Joseph M. Juran, Peter Drucker, Carmen Reihart, Kenneth Rogoff, and John Hope Franklin. Every page resonates with keenly applied and compassionate intelligence.

While the fluid prose lends itself to a quick, comfortable read, the sensitive nuanced portraits are unlike anything else readers are likely to have encountered. As such, they are meant to be savored. Because of its depth and extraordinary insight, these readings are not for the faint of heart: it will challenge readers at a deep level—particularly those who see themselves as already "successful." By revealing what these six leaders have experienced, what they think and feel, what they do—and, most important, how they have made their mark on the world—Bruce compels us to explore and perhaps redefine our vision of what constitutes success.

As a pragmatic ethicist with a background in finance, I see *Conquering Tomorrow Today: Six Exemplar Lives* as a fitting guide for taxed executives and driven professionals, offering a vision of how to choose to be what you truly are, by discovering that you have more innate courage than you may believe. The narratives of shared ethical accomplishment may be an "easy read," but they trace the twists and turns of a tough life mission.

D. V. Poole
Private Executive Advisory

Ongoing Global Issues

How is corporate America responding to the global COVID-19 outbreak and how are major multi-national corporations dealing with ongoing global issues such as climate change and economic inequality?

We spoke with best-selling business author and management consultant *Bruce Piasecki* to learn about the economic impact of the coronavirus pandemic on global corporations and how they are responding to the ongoing challenges.

In addition to being a sought-after speaker and leading management consultant, Dr. Piasecki is a best-selling author of a dozen books, including *Doing More With Less: The New Way to Wealth; Doing More With Teams; New World Companies: The Future of Capitalism and World Inc.*, which has been published in 10 foreign editions and has won several awards on globalization. In addition to his business books, Dr. Piasecki also wrote a memoir, *Missing Persons: A Life of Unexpected Influences*, which includes a foreword by author Jay Parini.

Dr. Bruce Piasecki earned his bachelor's and Ph.D. degrees from Cornell University and has run professional education and degree programs at Cornell, Clarkson University and Rensselaer Polytechnic University. At RPI, he developed one of the nation's first Master's of Science degree in Environmental Management and Policy.

Watch the Paul Grondahl / Dr. Bruce Piasecki interview at The Conversation.

https://www.nyswritersinstitute.org/post/the-economic-impact-of-the-pandemic-on-global-corporations

About the Author

Bruce Piasecki is the author of a dozen books, including the best seller *Doing More with Less*, and a memoir, *Missing Persons: A Life of Unexpected Influences*. He holds bachelor's and Ph.D. degrees from Cornell University and developed one of the nation's first Master's of Science degree in Environmental Management and Policy at RPI. He has lived in New York's Capital Region for over a quarter century with his wife and daughter.

www.doingmorewithlessbook.com

An excerpt from Piasecki's next Chapbook:
The Social Intelligence of Linda Coady

Deep Listening During Times
Of Social Panic

It is hard to imagine it. It was once common. Staging an Olympics. A big deal. You attract thousands of the world's elite athletes, their entourages, 40 to 60 corporate sponsors, hundreds of suppliers. It is a grand show, where millions of people watch what you've done on TV, with hundreds of thousands in attendance, enthralled.

The life of Linda Coady gave me an insider account of what it was like, during the days I was writing my book *Doing More with Teams*. Linda served as vice-president of sustainability for the Vancouver 2010 Olympics and is currently executive director of the Pembina Institute, an environmental think tank in Alberta. What matters now is how to "become like Linda" during these times of panic over racial riots, the Virus, and severe disruptive weather. And then for us to reassemble in our communities with dignity and a peaceful productivity.

Each modern Olympics involves building a moderate size city within an old city. "You buy and need practically everything," a Canadian health official told me "even enough Clorox disinfecting wipes to go around the world several times." How did Linda learn these social skills in our times of relentless social mischief and seriously inflamed divide?

What does the skills of creating an Olympics have to do with today's unrest? Now we all know that the world has become more volatile, because of shifting interests and human rights across the globe; that it appears more uncertain, both because of mass inequality and the impacts of climate change; and it has become more complex, because of the growing interdependence of business and society. Chris Coulter, the CEO of GlobeScan, calls these related features VUCA, as he suggests that the world has also grown more ambiguous "because our traditional governance and power structures are now unfit for this new more transparent age."

Yet I still know from experience that the skills found in Linda Coady are more timely than ever.

The Origins of Social Intelligence

The first time I asked Linda about the development of her skills, she said she came from two worlds: one of science and social leadership, and one of faith and virtues.

I asked Linda about her origins, she said one can learn a great deal by "listening through the differences between a father, a mother, and your siblings, let alone the range of people within your neighborhood — if you look long and hard at it each day."

Over dinner conversations, she absorbed from her father a sense of respect, social inclusion, and professionalism in debates. How doctors treat their particular spectrum of humanity with attention to detail is what Linda Coady has come to embody; a direct lineage, I trust, from father to daughter:

- Listen
- Be Careful
- Be Attentive
- Be Kind
- Solve Real Problems

Sure, all doctors have tons of data, reams of materials that show how your blood does not lie. But how a patient presents themselves, exactly like the protesters now in our cities, is the matter at hand. How a doctor hears what the patient presents is often the difference between life and death.

Linda Coady's mother kept order in a house of four children; and "was intelligent on how to navigate the world." I got the strong impression that her sisters and brothers were quite different, so I asked. Her youngest sister now teaches in the same Catholic school. Her other younger sister is a computer science professor at one of Canada's major universities. Her brother died early. All this readied Linda Coady to celebrate diversity, a trait we all need.

Such social wisdom survives the chaos of more data, more political positioning, more media surveillance, more techno-think about invading foreigners.

From the start, Linda said the second major influence in her life were the nuns at the Sisters of Charity of St. Louis. This teaching order of nuns ran the Catholic girl's school that first helped form Linda. It was in the range of 48 to 78 girls where Linda studied from 8th grade (when it first opened) to 12th grade.

"Here," she told me, "is where I realized things are not black and white, that fundamental human traits are discernible. The nuns emphasized the virtues over the vices. Here at school we were trained in humility, inclusion, and what excellence might be."

She added: "But I also learned from the Sisters something about the vices—the **vice of intolerance, the dangers of arrogance, the powerful distractions in adhering to the preoccupations with the self**." This active synthesis of Mom and Dad's worlds made her ready for a world of disinformation, lying, and basic self-interest.

"But," she reflected, "the greatest virtue the overall experience of growing up gave me is that to do my best requires focus. There is a fundamental human virtue in focus, the cultivated ability to bear down." The ability to bear down becomes a honed skill we need in times of social panic.

Our world at times seems to have lost these skills. We seem replete with one-sided stories, with needs taken out of context and magnified by social media. The world remains full of idle and selfish wheel-spinning. I cannot make too much of what I've learned from Linda Coady in the last decade. I think it fits the Capital Region, our national needs, as well as this spinning world where both the fears of George Orwell and the certainties of Donald Trump need to be reconciled daily. We need more Linda in our lives, not more Clorox, I fear.

CPSIA information can be obtained
at www.ICGtesting.com
Printed in the USA
BVHW091232011220
594381BV00004B/13